UNIVERSITY OF NORTH CAROLINA
STUDIES IN THE ROMANCE LANGUAGES AND LITERATURES
Number 98

CRITICAL REACTIONS AND THE CHRISTIAN ELEMENT
IN THE POETRY OF
PIERRE DE RONSARD

CRITICAL REACTIONS AND THE CHRISTIAN ELEMENT IN THE POETRY OF
PIERRE DE RONSARD

BY

MARK S. WHITNEY

WITH A FOREWORD BY

W. L. WILEY

CHAPEL HILL
THE UNIVERSITY OF NORTH CAROLINA PRESS

DEPÓSITO LEGAL: V. 959 - 1971

ARTES GRÁFICAS SOLER, S. A. - JÁVEA, 28 - VALENCIA (8) - 1971

TABLE OF CONTENTS

	Pages
FOREWORD	11
CRITICAL REACTIONS AND THE CHRISTIAN ELEMENT IN THE POETRY OF PIERRE DE RONSARD	15

The completion of this study was made possible by Summer Research Stipends in 1965 and 1966 from Brown University

FOREWORD

The first half of the French Renaissance — the period normally included by *seiziémistes* in the reign of Francis I (1515-1547) — might well be called pagan. It was a moment of intoxication with Greek and Roman antiquity, and of translating and editing ancient authors like Homer, Vergil, Euripides, and Seneca. It was an interlude during which the King himself, with little regard for the Christian Saints of an earlier era, paid homage to the nymph of Fontainebleau in a visit sketched by the Italian artist, Niccolo dell' Abbate. And, too, at the same time that he was doing expiation for the Affaire des Placards Francis I was having the palace of Fontainebleau decorated by the Italian masters, Primaticcio and Rosso, with the mythological figures of that most "dangerously alluring pagan" (an epithet of Professor E. K. Rand), Ovid. Despite its sporadic efforts at eliminating the ideas of Martin Luther and John Calvin, the early Renaissance in France looked back, then, for its poetic and artistic inspiration to the legacy of Greece and Rome.

The poets of the second half of the sixteenth century, during the regimes of Henri II and Charles IX, were inevitably more conscious than their immediate predecessors of the Protestant-Catholic conflict that would lead to the Wars of Religion and the Massacre of Saint Bartholomew; and, also, of the Council of Trent with its efforts at reform inside the Church of Rome and reestablishment of Papal powers. There was certainly no lessening at this time of interest in antiquity, and many poets, following the admonition of Du Bellay in the *Défense,* pillaged the ancients and brought the spoils home. However, it would scarcely have been possible for a poet — despite a deep indoctrination in classical lore — to have ignored the fact that he was living in a Christian world tragically torn asunder over its own interpretation of Christianity. It is in this framework that Professor Whitney has sought to reexamine some of the verse of the greatest of the French Renaissance poets, Pierre de Ronsard.

Ronsard's genius manifested itself in many directions. He could copy the formalized bombast of Pindar, the amorous frolicsomeness of Anacreon, the stylized ruralism of Horace in pursuit of a Bandusian spring, or Homeric and Vergilian grandeur in the ill-starred *Franciade*. Many modern readers have thought of Ronsard as being primarily a poet of love, an attitude more firmly entrenched in the early 1950's by Fernand Desonay's excellent study, *Ronsard poète de l'amour*. In more recent years the *baroquistes* have claimed the older Ronsard as one of their own, saying that in his later years he was no longer the "poète de l'amour et des roses" but rather the proponent of "Gothic" phenomena like demons, skeletons and death.[1] The many facets of Ronsard's poetry must be admitted, and Professor Whitney has legitimately taken another look at the Christian elements in the works of the Prince of Poets.

For his conclusions Professor Whitney has drawn primarily on Ronsard's *Hymnes*, and rather specific attention has been given the *Hymne de la Philosophie*, the *Hymne des Daimons*, the *Hymne du Ciel*, and the *Hymne de la Mort*. In the examination of the *Hymne de la Philosophie* it is quite aptly noted that Philosophy acts "not without a certain presumption" in usurping some of the functions of God. But, on this point, Ronsard must have remembered his Boethius and recalled that in the *Consolatio philosophiae* there was no real antipathy between Lady Philosophy and the Christian God. In the *Hymne de Daimons*, Professor Whitney finds a validity of Christian inspiration and not simply a restatement of medieval superstitions — although it is recognized that Ronsard was not unfamiliar with Neo-platonistic theories (as expressed in the *Enneads* of Plotinus) on the structure of the universe. With regard to the *Hymne des Daimons*, Professor Whitney is in disagreement with the critical conclusions of Gustave Cohen and Henri Franchet; there would be more of an accord on Whitney's part with the

---

[1] See Marcel Raymond, *Baroque et Renaissance poétique* (Paris: José Corti, 1955), p. 82 ff.

opinions of Henri Weber who thought that Christian elements were an integral segment of Ronsard's aesthetics.

In the *Hymne du Ciel,* despite its Platonic and Aristotelian allusions, there is found a major Christian content — and the *Ciel* is essentially the "haute maison de DIEU." The *Hymne de la Mort* is rightly considered by Professor Whitney as a primary statement of the Christian faith of Ronsard, since in it the poet moves from the pagan realms of Charon and Cerberus to the domains of Christ. From these four poems, and other examples of Ronsard's verse, Professor Whitney concludes that the Christian elements in the poet make an indispensable contribution to his greatness.

Professor Whitney quite legitimately calls attention once more to the Christian background of Ronsard, and he does it with a wealth of bibliography of previous scholarly opinion on the subject. Fortunately, it is not necessary for a Ronsard admirer to choose between the pagan Ronsard and the Christian Ronsard, since the Prince of Poets could couch his creations on either a pagan or Christian base. But it should be recalled that Ronsard remained loyal to the Church of Rome and that he hated the Huguenots — and all "ces noms qui sont finis en *os.*"

W. L. WILEY
Chapel Hill, N. C.

Ronsard's works having a Christian inspiration or orientation have elicited frequent and copious commentary from students of his life and poetic career. The following verses, for example, were clearly destined to evoke scholarly, critical, and even censorious attention:

> Quand au temple nous serons
> Agenouillés, nous ferons
> Les devots selon la guise
> De ceus qui pour loüer Dieu,
> Humbles se courbent au lieu
> Le plus secret de l'eglise.
>
> Mais quand au lit nous serons
> Entrelassés, nous ferons
> Les lascifs, selon les guises
> Des amans, qui librement
> Pratiquent folatrement
> Dans les dras cent mignardises.[1]

Verses like these are representative of a large body of Renaissance poetry where disparity and apparent contradiction in convention, theme, tone, and intention are often the rule. The hardy juxtaposition in the poem of sacred worship and sexual love, moreover, suggests the complex temperament of the author of the sensuous *Folastries*, the philosophical *Hymnes*, the polemic *Discours*, and the exquisite *Derniers Vers* remarkable for their profoundly moving expression of spiritual longing and of the poet's awareness of his vulnerable humanity and mortality. Furthermore, the inelegant,

---

[1] The six remaining stanzas, which continue in the vein of stanza 2, may be read in Paul Laumonier's critical edition of the *Œuvres complètes* (Paris: STFM, 1930), VI, 218-220. All references to Ronsard's works, unless otherwise indicated, are to this edition.

youthfully exuberant *Ode* of 1555 is not without importance for a fuller appreciation of the delicate balance achieved in the *Derniers Vers* between the Humanist's farewell to life and the dying man's yearning not only for deliverance from illness and pain but, also, for the soul's preservation or repose.[2]

The apparent naïveté and contradiction often encountered in Ronsard's works pertaining to the fundamental question of man's relationship to his creator have constituted an enduring problem for his critics. In respect to Ronsard's dual inspiration, the 'pagan,' or Humanistic, and the Christian, it now appears worthwhile to stress the fact that the presence of the Christian element in Ronsard's total production is not incidental to his main concerns either as a thinker or as a poet. The considerable body of Ronsard's verse exploiting Christian themes and images makes it desirable, also, to review at the present time some of the more important critical stances taken on the question of Ronsard's Christianity. Critical opinion is sharply divided on questions of fundamental importance for our understanding of Ronsard's use in crucially important poems of Christian themes and ideas and of the relationship of this element to his Humanism. The problem has not been adequately described, much less resolved, and it appears that we are far from a satisfactory evaluation of this aspect of his poetry and of how it bears upon the world view expressed in it.

It should be noted at the outset that in recent years the interpretation of Ronsard's thought has, with some important exceptions, tended to move away from a tradition accepting, if not always emphasizing, the genuineness and significance of the Christian inspiration at various times during his poetic career.[3] The

---

[2] Abbé F. Charbonnier describes the poem as one of the "exemples les plus frappants de ce mélange de christianisme et de paganisme" to be found in Ronsard's works (*La poésie française et les guerres de religion*, Paris, 1919, p. 435) and later comments on the duality of Ronsard's inspiration: "C'est bien le cas de dire avec M. Faguet [*Seizième Siècle, Etudes Littéraires*, Paris, n.d., p. xxxiii]: 'L'humaniste a deux hommes en lui, l'un pour lui et l'autre pour l'art, l'un qui est chrétien... qui va à Notre-Dame... l'autre qui est païen... qui adore Jupiter... et qui aime Glycère'" (p. 436). The seemingly bizarre morality is typical of a Renaissance mentality seeking to achieve in the here and now the best of two worlds or, at least, not to sacrifice entirely the one for the other.

[3] See, for example, Paul Laumonier, *Ronsard poète lyrique* (Paris, 1923), pp. 17-21, 233-234, 415-419, 498-499, 560-562, stressing the preeminence of

approach stressing Ronsard's evolution as a thinker toward rationalism and materialism [4] appears to have had as an article of faith that a considerable body of his hortatory and polemic poetry resulted from essentially nonreligious preoccupations: the political

---

the sensual, pagan, and materialistic predispositions of Ronsard or underlining the 'inappropriate' fusion of Christian and profane themes throughout the whole of Ronsard's lyric poetry, while not failing to acknowledge, however, the wholly Christian inspiration of poems like the *Hymne des pères de famille* and the unfinished *Hymne de Monsieur Sainct Roch* (pp. 267-269); Henri Busson, *Le rationalisme dans la littérature française* (Paris, 1957), pp. 362-393; Marc Bensimon, "Ronsard et la Mort," *MLR*, 57 (1962), 183-194, to mention only three of many critics opting ultimately for a pagan, rationalistic Ronsard. On the other hand, although Ronsard was in his own time roundly denounced as a pagan and an atheist, he also found his defenders: his biographer Binet, for example, and his eulogist Du Perron, whose description of the 'troubles in religion' shows "Ronsard as a great Catholic champion" (Frances Yates, *The French Academies of the Sixteenth Century*, London, 1947, p. 181). Among the modern critics favoring the view of a more authentic Christian inspiration, see Henri Weber: "Fidéisme et scepticisme," in his *La création poétique au seizième siècle en France* (Paris, 1956), pp. 49-52; Raymond Lebègue, *Ronsard* (Paris, 1961), pp. 62-65, 75-86, 140-143. For a succinct description of Ronsard's loyalism and religious conservatism in the light of the rapidly evolving politico-religious climate of 1560-1563, see also Laumonier's Introduction to the *Œuvres Complètes*, XI, v-xvii. Ronsard in his youth was sympathetic to the "préréformateurs" and "avait failli devenir protestant" (pp. v-vi). For what is undoubtedly the best statement to date on the cultural and literary meaning of Ronsard's Christianity, see Yates's chapter on "The Funeral of Ronsard" (*French Academies*, pp. 177-198) in which the poet's Christianity and paganism are viewed as thoroughly intermingled. More recently Frieda S. Brown has stressed the fear of anarchy and social chaos as basic to Ronsard's political and religious conservatism in her insightful "Interrelations between the Political Ideas of Ronsard and Montaigne" (*Romanic Review*, LVI, 1965, 241-247).

[4] Busson, for example, like most of Ronsard's critics, accepts the authenticity of the Christian inspiration of the *Hymnes* and other poems of the fifties: "Sa doctrine fut assez longtemps parfaitement orthodoxe. Que ce soit dans l'*Epitaphe de Jean Martin* (1553), dans celle de Loyse de Mailly (1554 environ), dans la *Prosopopée de Louys de Ronsard* (1554) ou dans l'*Hymne de la Mort*.... Non seulement Ronsard croit à l'immortalité chrétienne, mais il y croit en chrétien et non en philosophe" (*Le rationalisme*, pp. 381-382). The *Hymne de la Mort* is "admirable de pureté chrétienne, plus chrétien dans sa simplicité que les traités même des théologiens..." (p. 382). Nonetheless, Busson sees Ronsard as finally materialistic and evolving toward a kind of "panthéisme stoïcien" (p. 386): "un certain glissement au panthéisme, caractéristique du dernier tiers de la vie de Ronsard" (p. 365). Weber, on the other hand, views Ronsard's rationalism in a different light: "Faut-il penser que la tendance panthéiste d'une part, l'importance attribuée au corps de l'autre, font éclater la religion chrétienne de Ronsard? Nullement" (*Création poétique*, p. 49).

conservatism and opportunism of a court poet, respect for national traditions, and patriotism; and that these motivations preclude less worldly considerations on Ronsard's part. For these reasons Ronsard's alleged Christian faith is to be regarded with considerable caution, if not suspicion. [5] As for the ambitious and serious philoso-

---

[5] Suchier and Birch-Hirschfeld in their *Geschichte der franzoesischen Literatur* (Leipzig, 1900), p. 350, underline the role played by patriotism, Humanism, and loyalism in Ronsard's religious conservatism. Pierre Perdrizet in *Ronsard et la Réforme* (Paris, 1902), pp. 65-120, examines these motivations at length as well as those attributable to a court poet such as Ronsard. His conclusion that Ronsard's ultimate hostility to the Reformation was less the result of profound religious conviction than of his conservatism is for the most part acceptable also to Abbé Froger ("Ronsard et la Réforme," *Annales Fléchoises*, III, 1903, 276-289). Abbé Charbonnier expresses a similar, yet more qualified, opinion: "Pour expliquer l'attitude des poètes officiels, nous avons fait en son lieu la plus large part à l'esprit de courtisanerie, surtout en ce qui concerne le chef de la Pléiade. Mais ce serait mal connaître ce mouvement que de s'en tenir là.... Les causes de cette scission... sont d'ordre à la fois littéraire et religieux... le patriotisme est plutôt une conséquence qu'une cause de cette lutte..." (*La poésie française*, p. 379). Charbonnier also notes Ronsard's "tendance à la modération," that "il avait fallu le déchaînement de la guerre civile" before he was seized by "l'ivresse du sang," and that "tout cela n'empêche le grand humaniste de reconnaître à plusieurs de ses adversaires le mérite de la bonne foi, de la sincérité religieuse" (p. 386). Ronsard's famous Catholic credo is viewed sympathetically, yet his principal objection to the Reformation is explained by his opposition of the principle of authority and spirit of tradition to independent reason and the authority of the Bible alone (pp. 390-392): "Tel est le grief fondamental qu'il a contre l'église réformée. Il ne cesse d'invoquer pour lui 'la foy de ses ayeuls' et il se moque des femmelettes et des enfants qui se mêlent d'enseigner la parole de Dieu." Fully stated, however, is the awkwardness of the position of a "chanoine grassement prébendé [qui] faisait le jeu de ses adversaires, qui se disaient précisément envoyés pour ramener l'Eglise de Jésus-Christ à sa simplicité et à sa pauvreté primitives" (pp. 393-394). Charbonnier indicates the fundamental reasons for Ronsard's scepticism and fideism: "Voilà Ronsard aux antipodes du rationalisme protestant, de cet esprit critique qui est au fond du système calviniste. Il a tellement pris en horreur la manie de la dispute et du libre examen, qu'il préconise la foi aveugle, celle des humbles et des ignorants. Il n'admet l'intervention de la raison que dans les sciences qui ne touchent pas à Dieu" (pp. 396-397). Finally, Ronsard's juxtaposition of pagan and Christian subjects as in the *Hercule Chrestien* is regarded as an "irrévérence" (p. 435). In this respect, Charbonnier's characterization of the 16th century's imperfect syncretism of the Christian and the pagan is typical of much current thinking: "On le voit, l'erreur est profonde. Les mythes anciens ne pouvaient tels quels servir de cadre à l'inspiration chrétienne; il fallait au naturalisme antique une transformation beaucoup plus radicale, pour ne pas heurter de front la conscience religieuse moderne. A travers les graces sensuelles de l'art païen,

phical poetry, the view that the Christian faith is essentially foreign to Ronsard's Humanism as well as to his poetic temperament has found support in the massive research into his use of the works of classical poets and philosophers, which demonstrates the great multiplicity of influences as well as the protean inspiration and nature of Ronsard's philosophical attitudes. The conclusion appears to be that the incorporation of Christian themes into his work is incidental or only sporadically related to his main concerns, if not atypical. [6]

Despite the studies of Catholic critics like Le Sage and the measured prudence of *Ronsardisants* such as Weber and Lebègue, [7] the continuing and wholly valid concern with Ronsard's Humanism has tended to obscure the curious role played by the Christian element in his poetry. The increasing emphasis on the number and variety of Ronsard's sources encourages a fragmented view of his metaphysical and religious poetry as being to a large extent a kind of passive repository, or mirror, of the ideas of various schools or movements. [8] The inference, of course, is that Ronsard's poetry in this respect may lack focus and cohesion. The kind of fragmentation to which I refer inevitably results in conclusions stressing an eclecticism on Ronsard's part departing significantly from a Christian view of man and of man's condition. [9] The alternatives would

---

le sentiment chrétien ne pouvait se faire jour qu'en lui infusant une lumière, une vie toute nouvelle. Ce travail de transformation allait commencer avec la 'poésie militante' et se continuer, à l'âge classique, avec *Polyeucte* de Corneille, *Athalie* de Racine, en attendant la rénovation romantique. Au XVIe siècle, pour tirer nos poètes de l'imitation servile de leurs modèles, soit bibliques, soit mythologiques, il ne fallait rien moins que la secousse des guerres religieuses" (p. 438).

[6] This line of reasoning explains, perhaps, a certain caution in emphasizing the significance of the authenticity and durability of Ronsard's Christian inspiration even in respect to passages where a genuine Christian orientation is totally explicit. See, for example, Isidore Silver, "Ronsard's Ethical Thought," *BHR*, XXIV (1962), 88-117, 339-374.

[7] See nn. 3, 4 and, also, Abbé Müller, *La poésie religieuse catholique de Marot à Malherbe* (Paris, 1950).

[8] See, for example, Henry Hornik's "More on Ronsard's Philosophy: The Hymns and Neoplatonism," *BHR*, XXVII (1965), 435-443.

[9] "Laumonier's insistence upon Ronsard's traditionalism in the *Hymnes* seems to be contradicted by the poet's syncretism. Whatever his immediate sources, Ronsard adapted them to suit his own poetic expression. Busson's and Silver's conclusion that his cosmology is, at one stage, syncretically platonic is more justified by the evidence" (Hornik, p. 442).

appear to be to revive the Huguenots' charges of atheism, blasphemy, and cynical hypocrisy, or to put Ronsard down as a hopelessly confused and confusing thinker. [10]

The gallery of portraits in respect to Ronsard the thinker is bewildering. In it we have already found the Neoplatonist, the pagan,

---

[10] Sainte-Beuve, without explicitly calling Ronsard's religious sincerity into question, expressed dissatisfaction at the *Hymnes*' eclecticism and their confused alliance of incompatible traditions: "La mythologie la plus savante, des allégories astronomiques perpétuelles, un mélange confus de platonisme et de christianisme, font pour nous de ces poèmes si admirés en leur temps une lecture presque inintelligible et parfaitement ennuyeuse. Ronsard a essayé de consacrer ce genre païen aux saints de l'église; il a célébré saint Blaise et saint Roch, mais l'essai n'a pas été heureux, et dans ses préoccupations classiques il est allé parler à saint Roch de *Lucine* et d'*Hyménée*" (*Œuvres choisies de Pierre de Ronsard*, Paris, 1828, p. 275). Sainte-Beuve, like Perdrizet and Charbonnier almost a full century later, stressed the other than religious motivation of the polemical *Discours* in which Ronsard is most vulnerable to charges of cynicism and self-seeking: "Dans les sanglantes querelles du seizième siècle, Ronsard prit le parti de la cour et de la religion catholique. Nourri des bienfaits de Henri II, de Catherine de Médicis et de ses fils, il avait encore pour motif de ce choix l'amour du loisir et de la paix, qui inspira également Horace et Malherbe. La haine que portaient les huguenots aux lettres profanes et aux frivolités galantes devait aussi l'indisposer contre eux. ... Il faut dire, à l'honneur de Ronsard, que toutes ces pièces respirent, au milieu de préventions injustes, une profonde horreur des troubles, une tendre et filiale piété pour la France" (p. 309). The way is, thus, well paved for the modern critic's hesitation to seek a construct capable of reconciling the pagan with the Christian Ronsard. Gustave Cohen, for example, in his study of the *Hymnes* and *Discours* (*Ronsard, sa vie et son œuvre*, 3rd ed., Paris, 1956) limits himself to noting the 'contradictions' and questioning their meaning: "Ah! le beau vers! [*Hymne de la Mort*: 'Et de mourir pour Luy, comme il est mort pour nous']. Mais pourquoi parler ensuite d'Ixion, de Tantale, de Charon, du chien Cerbère 'à trois abbois', dont le sang de Jésus nous affranchit?" (p. 173). Later on Cohen again minimizes the importance of Ronsard's Christianity when, speaking of the apparent "élément purement chrétien" of the *Hymne du Ciel*, he states that there is also "plus de christianisme que de paganisme, en dépit du titre, qui implique un partage à doses égales, dans *L'Hercule chrestien*" (p. 177). He concludes that "ce ne sont là que des essais de fonder une poésie de plus vaste envergure et moins assujettie à un original et à un accompagnement musical que les *Psaumes* de Marot. On ne pourra guère, en dépit de quelques beaux vers que nous avons cités, affirmer que Ronsard fut un grand poète chrétien" (p. 178). Further on, however, Cohen adds: En relisant ce passage [the profession of faith in *Responce aux injures* (XI, 135-137)] où l'élévation de la pensée le dispute à la simplicité et à l'ampleur de la période, nous serons amenés à nous demander si nous avons bien fait d'hésiter à reconnaître en Ronsard un grand poète chrétien" (p. 209)!

materialist, rationalist, pantheist, and stoic.[11] There has been, on the other hand, a growing, more fully articulated awareness of the need for renewed emphasis on the aesthetic approach to the reconciliation of apparent contradictions in Ronsard's poetry.[12] Little light is shed upon what Ronsard intended and actually achieved in his poetry by the tendency to elaborate on the poet's supposed cynicism in his overt espousal of the Catholic cause and in his repeated avowals of abiding faith and orthodoxy. A more meaningful appraisal may be gained through an aesthetic approach combined with a heightened awareness of the long-standing tradition of Christian Humanism's incorporation of the wisdom and beauty of pagan antiquity into a Christian view of man and his place in the universe.[13]

We can, today, affirm with no more demonstrable certainty the ultimate quality of Ronsard's faith than could his 16th-century Protestant detractors:

> O pauvres abusez! que le cuider sçavoir
> Plus que toute l'Eglise, a laissé decevoir:
> Tenez vous en vos peaux, & ne jugez personne,
> Je suis ce que je suis, ma conscience est bonne,
> Et Dieu, à qui le cœur des hommes apparoist,
> Sonde ma volunté, & seul il la connoist.
>
> (*Elégie à Loïs des Masures*, X, 364)

Yet, despite Ronsard's penchant for extravagance and hyperbole in his numerous protestations of orthodox belief, his poetry, the end product of his erudition and poetic genius, by the very breath that animates it is not an insignificant document:

> Or ce Dieu tout parfait, plain d'eternelle essence,
> Tout remply de vertu, de bonté, de puissance,
> D'immence majesté, qui voit tout, qui scait tout,

---

[11] See above, nn. 2, 3, 4.

[12] Henri Weber, for example, sees Ronsard's syncretism as containing a genuine Christian element and his fusion of disparate traditions as a truly poetic function (*Création poétique*, pp. 60-62).

[13] Even "der erste humanistische Dichter Frankreichs," Jean Lemaire de Belges, in spite of his bedazzlement by pagan antiquity, as early as 1509 gives signs of the secular 16th-century French Humanist's participation in the medieval tradition of Christian and pagan syncretism. See my review of P. Jodogne, ed. Jean Lemaire de Belges, *La Concorde du genre humain* (Bruxelles, 1964), *RP*, XXII (1968), 99-103.

> Sans nul commencement, sans milieu, ne sans bout,
> Dont la divinité tresroyalle & supresme
> N'a besoin d'autre bien, sinon de son bien mesme,
> Se commençant par elle & finissant en soy :
> Bref ce Prince eternel, ce Seigneur & ce Roy,
> Qui des peuples le pere & le pasteur se nomme,
> Ayant compassion des miseres de l'homme,
> Et desirant qu'il fust du peché triomphant,
> En ce monde envoya son cher unique Enfant,
> Eternel comme luy, de la mesme matiere,
> Ayant du pere sien la gloire toute entiere.
>
> (*Responce aux injures*, XI, 135-136)

Relevant, too, are such poems as the *Hercule Chrestien* (1555), published eight years before the *Responce*. The former poem has been viewed both as an earnest attempt to reconcile the Christian and pagan cultures, to effect a *concorde* between the two, with each lending the other its validity and prestige, and as a shocking mélange of mutually exclusive beliefs and systems of thought.[14] Many other

---

[14] Laumonier's notes to the *Hercule chrestien* (VIII, 206-224) clearly demonstrate the division of opinion on this point from the 16th century on beginning with Nicolas Denisot's approbative prefatory sonnet of 1555 (VIII, 206-207) and the condemnations of protestants like Florent Chrestien whose *Seconde responce de F. la Baronie* (1563) describes the poem as blasphemous and proof of Ronsard's atheism (VIII, 223, n. 1). Laumonier further notes Besly's correction (1604) of Chrestien in pointing to the centuries-old tradition of such assimilations. References to Guillaume Budé's comparisons of Christ to Hercules (*De Asse*, 1515), the bishop of Limoges' erecting in his cathedral of a rood screen depicting the labors of Hercules as prefiguring those of Christ, and Denisot's presentation in a *Cantique* (1553) of Hercules strangling the serpent in his cradle as a symbol of the infant Jesus fully justify Laumonier's conclusion that Ronsard "ne faisait donc... que suivre une tradition ininterrompue" (pp. 223-224, n. 1). No one, however, had as yet "poursuivi le parallélisme entre les deux hommes-dieux aussi loin que lui, et l'on comprend que certains rapprochements... aient passé pour une profanation aux yeux des chrétiens réformés" (loc. cit.). Marcel Simon in his *Hercule et le Christianisme* (Strasbourg, 1955) follows Laumonier and, referring to Denisot and Marguerite de Navarre, states a general 16th-century exegetical principle : "Il consiste à étendre à la mythologie païenne, conçue comme source ou à tout le moins reflet d'une révélation, les méthodes d'interprétation que la théologie chrétienne applique à l'Ancien Testament" (p. 183). Ronsard substitutes "à la simple allégorie la typologie, et cherche dans les épisodes du mythe non plus l'expression symbolique de vérités philosophiques ou morales, mais l'annonce de faits historiques, la préfiguration de l'Evangile" (p. 184) so that, as in Michelangelo's Last Judgment and Zelotti's frescoes of Villa Emo, "la jonction est faite entre la révélation

passages of the *Hymnes,* the polemic poems, epitaphs, and so on evoking the Christian Deity, relegating the pagan divinities to the status of reifications of *DIEU*'s manifold attributes, expressing the poet's orthodoxy, or describing his piously spent day may be viewed

---

biblique et la tradition des Gentils" (p. 184). Trousson in "Ronsard et la légende d'Hercule," *BHR,* XXIV (1962) likewise views the poem in the broader perspective and emphasizes the originality of Ronsard, one of the first to effect "l'assimilation complète d'un symbole mythologique aux doctrines chrétiennes" (p. 85) and "l'assimilation la plus complète des thèmes mythologiques aux thèmes bibliques..." (p. 86). Thus, the poet is "un témoin important de la transmutation des formes de pensée: continuant la tradition fondée par Annius de Viterbe et Jacques de Bergame, il prépare le renouveau de l'exégèse biblique au début du XVIIᵉ siècle et préfigure les arguments des Samuel Bochart et des Vossius. Il marque, enfin, la rupture définitive avec l'évhémérisme médiéval" (p. 87). Underscored once again, then, is the intrinsic complexity and importance of Ronsard's Christianity. Clear, too, is the nature of the extreme positions taken on either side of the question. Cohen, for example, sees the Humanist's poem as but "une concession singulière à la méthode d'interprétation médiévale et scolastique..." (*Ronsard,* p. 177). Pierre de Nolhac long ago noted the enduring syncretic tradition: " 'Hercule chrétien', désignation qui s'applique, suivant les formules usitées par l'humanisme du temps, à Jésus-Christ lui-même," and hypothesized that the "pieux poème semble, par le rapprochement des dates, une sorte de rachat des *Folastries*" ("Documents nouveaux sur la Pléiade: Ronsard, Du Bellay," *RHLF,* 1899, p. 358). Even earlier, Dupré in his "Ronsard, poète chrétien," *Congrès archéologique* (Angers, 1872) had expressed a similar theory, especially in respect to the pious beginning of the poem: "C'était, sans doute, la voix du remords qui parlait ainsi à une conscience déjà chargée de nombreuses peccadilles et rien moins que tranquille" (p. 560). For Dupré, too, Ronsard in the final analysis was writing in a well-established, viable tradition acceptable to sympathetic contemporaries. This is evident in Ronsard's 17th-century editor's "Epitre dédicatoire de Nicolas Richelet à messire Charles de Balzac" (*Œuvres,* Paris: Buon, 1617, p. 1079): "L'Hercule païen est une fiction anticipée de ce que les prophètes et sibilles avoient figuré de l'Homme-Dieu nostre Seigneur Jésus-Christ. Et, pour cela, nostre poète a pris le sujet pour vendiquer du paganisme ce qui appartient proprement aux chrestiens" (quoted by Dupré, p. 561). Perdrizet, who also quotes from the "Epitre dédicatoire," accepts the alleged incompatibility of the two traditions and the Protestants' charge of atheism and makes a more severe judgment: "les protestants avaient raison contre Ronsard; ils avaient même raison d'autant plus que Ronsard se croyait tout à fait innocent, et qu'il ne sentait pas l'inconvenance de l'hymne dont la piété huguenote était justement blessée" (*Ronsard et la Réforme,* pp. 62-63). Charbonnier, as already noted (*supra,* n. 5), calls the poem an "irrévérence" and mentions other inappropriate mélanges to be found in Ronsard (*La poésie française,* pp. 435-436). Laumonier in 1923 describes it as a typical example of the "mélange bizarre de paganisme et de christianisme" (*Ronsard poète lyrique,* p. 418), while Chamard calls it, despite the verses celebrating "en beaux accents lyriques les louanges du Seigneur," an "œuvre malheureuse" (*Histoire,* II, 197-198).

as manifestations, to which varying degrees of importance may be assigned, of a continuing and essential concern with the Christian tradition into which he was born. The significance of the Christian element in Ronsard's poetry, indeed, is apparent in the sole fact of the large number of poems having a Christian inspiration or genuine relationship to Christian preoccupations and themes.[15]

Interestingly enough, at the preliminary stage of identifying the Christian poems we encounter the kind of divergence of critical opinion that characterizes discussion of the question of Ronsard's religion. Henri La Maynardière (Adrien Van Bever) in his anthology[16] selects eleven poems as most representative, one assumes, of Ronsard's Christian poetry: "O Seigneur Dieu, nous te louons" (1565), *Hymne des Pères de Famille sur le chant*: *Te rogamus audi nos*: "Sainct Blaise, qui vit aux cieux" (1587), *Hymne de Sainct Roch*: "Sus serrons-nous les mains" (1587), *Hymne à Saint Gervais et Saint Protais*: "La victorieuse couronne, Martyrs" (1550),[17] *Remonstrance au peuple de France* (1563), and six of the nine poems of the *Derniers Vers*: "Je n'ay plus que les os," "Donne moy tes

---

On the other hand, Abbé Sage claims that such opinions are based on a "défaut d'information historique" ("L'Hercule chrétien," résumé, Association Guillaume Budé, Congrès de Lyon. 8-13 septembre 1958. Actes du Congrès, Paris, 1960, p. 442) and concludes: "Voilà dans quelle longue suite de pensée 'théologique' et d'histoire spirituelle se placent Ronsard et son poème. Nicolas Denisot y a vu avec raison une preuve péremptoire des sentiments catholiques de l'auteur des *Odes* et des *Hymnes*, qu'il était injuste de damner sur ses *Gayetez* et ses *Folastries*. ... C'est qu'il n'y a rien de plus conforme au génie profond du catholicisme que cette annexion et cette intégration des valeurs spirituelles authentiques, même et surtout s'il faut les sauver d'un mélange vicieux" (p. 444).

[15] No attempt will be made here to establish the complete catalogue of such passages. Suffice it to say, as an indication of their importance, that I have already compiled a list of over 100 of Ronsard's poems referred to by critics interested in the problem of his Christianity. These poems span almost all of Ronsard's poetic career from near the beginning: *Avant-entrée du Roi treschrestien à Paris, Hymne de France* (1549) to the very end: *Hymne de Saint Roch, Derniers Vers*, "Les Hymnes sont des grecs...," *Fragment d'un poeme de la loy divine*. Thus, on purely chronological grounds, views such as Busson's stressing an evolution toward a kind of stoical materialism, though they admit of the authenticity of the Christian element in the earlier works (especially in some of the *Hymnes* of 1555), are subject to considerable revision.

[16] *Poètes chrétiens du XVIe siècle* (Paris, 1908).

[17] A few critics — Dupré and Charbonnier, for example — restrict Ronsard's 'purely' Christian poetry to these four poems.

presens," "Ah! longues nuicts d'hyver," "Quoy mon ame," "Il faut laisser maisons," *Le Tombeau de l'auteur composé par luy mesme*: "Ronsard repose icy." At the same time La Maynardière presents Ronsard's Catholicism and "fin chrétienne" in an all too favorable light, claiming for the poet not only a penchant "à la tradition et à l'obéissance catholique" (p. 142) but, also and throwing all reason to the winds, a "désintéressement jusqu'à asservir ses moindres desseins à la cause d'un peuple et d'une croyance" (p. 141), and a "foi catholique tout entière, puisqu'elle n'autorisait ni examen, ni murmure" (p. 141). He goes on to say with equal lack of restraint that "c'est là sa pensée; ce fut là toute sa vie. Communion intime de l'esprit et du dogme" (p. 141).

Pierre de Nolhac also makes a less than objective selection.[18] He groups without comment under the somewhat imprecise title, "La Religion" (pp. 277-305), extracts from the polemic literature and related poems: *Elégie à Guillaume des Autels* (1560): Ronsard on the "Abus de l'Eglise" (p. 279); *Discours à Louis des Masures*: in defense of his own faith, knowable to God alone; *Continuation du Discours des Misères* (1562): reply to charge of atheism and appeal to Théodore de Bèze; *Responce aux injures* (1563): Ronsard's "Profession de Foi Catholique" (p. 283). These are preceded by "Les Hymnes sont des Grecs invention première" of the posthumous *Œuvres* (1587),[19] by the sonnet: "Quelle nouvelle fleur apparaît à nos yeux" (1562), addressed to Anne de Marguets, the Poissy nun whom Ronsard describes as the "divinely" created

---

[18] In his otherwise excellent *Poésies choisies de Ronsard* (Paris, 1954).

[19] Worthy of note in the poem is Ronsard's preoccupation with fusing Humanism and Christianity as the following verses demonstrate:

> Ha, les Chrétiens devraient les Gentils imiter
> A couvrir de beaux lis et de roses leurs têtes,
> Et chômer tous les ans à certains jours de fêtes
> La mémoire et les faits de nos Saints immortels,
> Et chanter tout le jour autour de leurs autels,
> Vendre au peuple dévot pains d'épices et foaces,
> Défoncer les tonneaux, fêter les Dédicaces,
> Les hautbois enroués sonner branles nouveaux,
> Les villageois mi-bus danser sous les ormeaux,
> Tout ainsi que David sautait autour de l'Arche
> Sauter devant l'Image, et d'un pied qui démarche
> Sous le son du cornet, se tenant par les mains,
> Solenniser la fête en l'honneur de nos Saints.

(*Pierre de Nolhac*, p. 277)

flower of Poissy: "Aussi Dieu pour miracle en ce monde l'a mise, / Son printemps est le ciel, sa racine est l'Eglise, / Sa foi et œuvres sont ses feuilles et son fruit" (p. 278), and by the sonnet written twelve years later on the death of Charles IX. The last for its forceful expression of the Christian view of death requires quotation in full:

> Si le grain de froment ne se pourrit en terre,
> Il ne saurait porter ni feuille ni bon fruit;
> De la corruption la naissance se suit
> Et comme deux anneaux l'un en l'autre s'enserre.
> Le Chrétien endormi sous le tombeau de pierre
> Doit revêtir son corps en dépit de la nuit;
> Il doit suivre son Christ, qui la Mort a détruit,
> Premier victorieux d'une si forte guerre.
> Il vit assis là-haut, triomphant de la Mort;
> Il a vaincu Satan, les Enfers et leur Fort,
> Et a fait que la Mort n'est plus rien qu'un passage,
> Qui ne doit aux Chrétiens se montrer odieux,
> Auquel Charle' est passé pour s'envoler aux Cieux,
> Prenant pour lui le gain, nous laissant le dommage.
>
>   (*Pierre de Nolhac*, pp. 278-279)[20]

Nolhac's notion, however, of Ronsard's religious thought is revealed in his inclusion, under such titles as "La Mythologie" (pp. 213-234), "La Philosophie" (pp. 235-254), and "La Nature" (pp. 169-185), of a number of passages that have long been in dispute in respect to the ultimate value of their Christian element.[21] Nolhac's headings legitimately underscore the diversity of Ronsard's interests and inspiration, yet they also imply a minimization of the importance of the Christian element. The thematic approach to the body of

---

[20] The sonnet intriguingly prefigures the more pessimistic, yet still Christian, tercets of the *Derniers Vers'* "Il faut laisser maisons..." and the more tempered conclusion of his self-composed epitaph:

> Ronsard repose icy qui hardy dés enfance
> Détourna d'Helicon les Muses en la France,
> Suivant le son du luth & les traits d'Apollon:
> Mais peu valut sa Muse encontre l'eguillon
> De la mort, qui cruelle en ce tombeau l'enserre,
> Son ame soit à Dieu, son corps soit à la terre.
>   (XVIII, 181)

[21] The *Hymne des Daimons*, for example, is found under "La Mythologie"; the *Hymne de la Mort* under "La Philosophie," and so on.

Ronsard's work as well as the impression of fragmentation and compartmentalization created by the emphasis on the variety and multiplicity of the sources tends to obscure the role of the Christian element in the total context of his poetry. The result is typical of general evaluations and representations of Ronsard's thought, preoccupations, and goals. Characteristic, too, is Nolhac's insistence upon ignoring the Christian inspiration in such philosophical and religious poems as, in addition to the *Hymnes* on Demons, Death, and Philosophy, the *Hymne de l'Eternité,* the *Hercule Chrestien,* and the *Hymne de la Justice.* More surprisingly, but still characteristically, the *Derniers Vers* are presented simply as "Vers Biographiques" (pp. 484-485).

There is, of course, a considerable body of occasional verse, epitaphs, and so on that relates to the theme of Ronsard's Christianity. Numerous philosophical poems, e.g., *Elégie à Robert de la Haye* (1560) and *Le Chat* (1569), among other poems frequently cited in support of Ronsard's pantheism, pessimism, materialism, or superstition, have inevitable theological consequences for Ronsard's thought and rarely is the Christian God totally removed from consideration in them. [22] This presence of the Christian element cannot adequately be accounted for by simple reference to the pervasively Christian atmosphere of Ronsard's day. [23] Ronsard's epitaphs, for example, though not abounding in Christian passages going clearly beyond mere lip service to custom, contain significant developments such as the whole of the *Epitaphe de Loyse de Mailly* (1555). [24] Such a poem is much less likely to leave the modern reader with the feeling of having read a bizarre and ultimately self-contradictory reconciliation of Christian and pagan themes than, say, the notorious *Hercule Chrestien.* Just as some of the sonnets

---

[22] There are numerous poems and passages of the like, some of which have already been referred to. Others will be cited as the occasion warrants. It is necessary to add, also, that as of now no attempt has been made to trace the chronological development and occurrence of the Christian element in Ronsard's works. Such an approach appears desirable despite the manifest complexity resulting from the continuing presence of this element in forms which both in thought and in genre are not greatly suggestive of an abandonment of successive pagan enthusiasms.

[23] For a statement of this point of view, see Lucien Febvre, *Le problème de l'incroyance au XVIe siècle* (Paris, 1947), p. 363.

[24] "Ou soit que la fortune, ou soit que le chemin..." (VIII, 229-234).

of the *Derniers Vers,* which contain moving exhortations to the soul to depart this life of torment and to follow the painful path traced by Christ, may not casually be dismissed as unrepresentative of Ronsard, so, too, the *Epitaphe* reveals to us a poet haunted by the dilemma of man's imperfect condition and his yearning to resolve it in terms permitting the reconciliation of the worlds of the spirit and of the flesh. It is noteworthy that in the poem Ronsard attempts not a choice but a union, that he does not here eschew the Christian faith, and that this appears not to be accounted for fully by the facts of his political circumstances and motivation. At times the reconciliations, typical as they are of the time, may appear artificial, forced, even ludicrous; others, however, are complete and emotionally, poetically, and aesthetically satisfying as when the poet, bidding Louise adieu, evokes an eternity of earthly as well as heavenly life upon the very threshold of death itself:

> Or adieu de rechef, adieu doncques LOYSE :
> A fin que ta memoire en oubly ne soit mise,
> Et que de mieux en mieux les siecles avenir
> De tes belles vertus se puissent souvenir,
> Soit printemps, soit esté, soit yver, tousjours tombe
> Une pluie d'œilletz & de lys sur ta tombe
> Menu comme rosée, & nuict & jour du Ciel
> Y puisse choir la manne, & s'y faire le miel.
>
> (VIII, 234)

The unique quality of Ronsard's religion and its expression is apparent in these verses. It is this quality, paradoxically perhaps, that is often obscured in the polemic poetry directed against the Protestants.[25] The philosophical poetry, too, although frequently and explicitly incorporating an orthodox Christianity, is marred by hesitation, contradiction, expediency, and outside, contingent influences of various kinds. Yet the two worlds of Ronsard fuse on occasion, without creating suspicion as to his motivation, into a new poetic reality, a reality not existing wholly outside of the poet's broad religious heritage. We may also note that in addition to the natural starting point provided by the *Epitaphes* for the seeker of

---

[25] Curiously, the latter works are credited by some — especially Charbonnier — with the introduction of meaningful Christian themes into Ronsard's poetry.

religious themes numerous other poems may be culled with substantial results. Much of the Platonic material, for example, which receives at Ronsard's hands an astonishing variety of application from amatory poetry to musings on the origin and order of the universe, is, inherently, in frequent harmony with the dualistic Christian view of man and his condition. [26]

Although we now have a keener appreciation of the presence of the Christian inspiration in Ronsard thanks to the recent contributions of Lebègue and Frappier, [27] much is still to be gained by pointing out representative poems and passages that have elicited considerable critical discussion in this respect and by attempting to show at what stage we have presently arrived in the evaluation of this highly significant element in Ronsard's poetry. Logic and economy require, however, for the time being that we leave entirely aside the continual echoes and commonplaces from Christian literature that one would expect to find in the work of any not actively antichristian poet of Ronsard's time.

One of the early critics to concentrate on the problem of Ronsard's Christianity, André Dupré, consistently and naively accepts the authenticity of his Christianity in whatever context it occurs. [28] Yet he readily acknowledges what for him is the disturbing

---

[26] On this point C. Ackermann's *The Christian Element in Plato*, trans. Samuel Ralph Asbury (Edinburgh, 1861) is useful, especially in the chapter on "That Which is Clearly Christian in Plato and his Philosophy" (pp. 231-251).

[27] See, for example, Lebègue's "Appendice" to Laumonier's edition of the *Œuvres* (VIII, 361-374) and Frappier's "L'Inspiration biblique et théologique de Ronsard dans *L'Hymne de la Justice*," *Mélanges d'histoire littéraire de la Renaissance offerts à Henri Chamard* (Paris, 1951), pp. 97-108.

[28] It is interesting to note that studies devoted exclusively, or importantly, to the subject are rare indeed. Aside from the works dealing specifically with the political origins and implications of Ronsard's polemic with the Protestants, we find Abbé Müller in his *La poésie religieuse* expressing a view which is essentially the same as Dupré's. Müller, significantly enough, rejects (p. 153, n. 5) the implications of Laumonier's description of Ronsard's Catholicism as the easy one of a "viveur paganisant... [qui] ne pouvait trouver une paix relative et pratiquer une vertu aisée que dans les rangs des Catholiques" (*Ronsard poète lyrique*, p. 225). Like Dupré, Müller also goes too far in accepting as genuine the Christian inspiration not only of Ronsard's disinterested productions but, also, of the *œuvres de combat* containing passages "inexplicables si l'on rejette la sincérité du poète. Ils semblent même beaucoup plus expressifs que la profession de foi en Dieu, en Jésus-Christ et en l'Eglise, de *la Response de 1563*" (p. 154, n. 2). Müller

presence of the pagan influence on Ronsard and his time: "Ce titre [*Ronsard, poète chrétien*] pourra sembler d'abord un paradoxe. Ronsard, en effet, est surtout célèbre par ses poésies profanes, voire même érotiques. Cet Anacréon ou, si l'on veut, cet Ovide moderne, a chanté de préférence, les passions volages dont il avait ressenti les dangereuses atteintes. Des idoles de chair et de sang furent les objets les plus ordinaires de ses tendres hommages. D'ailleurs, son talent, éclos en plein siècle, a subi nécessairement l'influence générale de l'époque. Nourri des auteurs grecs et latins, il puise habituellement ses inspirations aux sources païennes et fait un usage continuel de la mythologie. Dans ses ingénieuses fictions les mensonges de l'Olympe remplacent presque toujours les vérités du Christianisme." [29] Indeed, Dupré willingly, if mistakenly, lends credence to the sweeping characterization of the Renaissance itself as in large part not only irreligious but profane, idolatrous, and antichristian as well: "Le monde des lettres et des arts semblait alors avoir pris à tache de rétablir le culte des faux dieux et de faire oublier en quelque sorte la croix du Sauveur" (p. 555). Dupré's modest intention, despite the dogmatic tone of the title, is to reveal how "quelques vestiges des anciennes croyances" or "souvenirs indélébiles d'une éducation foncièrement chrétienne reprenaient le dessus, de temps à autre, et paraissaient ramener au bien les intelligences dévoyées ou les imaginations vagabondes. Nous voudrions rechercher dans les écrits du poète vendômois ces preuves clairsemées d'une foi assoupie, mais non atteinte" (p. 555).

The main arguments put forth by Dupré and which continue to have some relevance today in favor of the authenticity of Ronsard's Christianity may be summed up briefly: 1) Ronsard was a Christian by family and by national tradition (pp. 556-557), 2) his alleged priesthood, being a fiction of his Protestant adversaries, has no bearing on his ultimate sincerity in that he was in every way an

---

thus repeats for the most part a judgment made some 270 years ago by the obscure Isaac Ballart who, railing against the Protestants, "ces réformateurs prétendus de la Religion aigris de l'obstacle qu'il [Ronsard] apportait à leurs sinistres desseins," extolled the "innocence" of "ce grand homme [qui] ne méritait pas seulement le titre de poète français, mais encore de *poète chrétien*" (*Académie des sciences et des arts*, Bruxelles, 1695, II, 347. Cited by Dupré, p. 568).

[29] "Ronsard, poète chrétien," p. 554.

unremarkable participant, in so far as his personal life was concerned, in the well-established tradition of *clerc* entitled to various ecclesiastical benefits having little more than *pro forma* restrictions on his personal life, 3) in spite of his irregular behavior, penchant for gallantry, susceptibility to the attractions of court life, his self-seeking flattery of the great and the powerful, and so on through the mournful litany of our poet's transgressions, he remained always "attaché de cœur, sinon de conduite, à la foi de ses pères" (p. 557) and, when the time came, ready to undertake a warm defense of Catholicism in the *Discours des Misères,* dedicated to Catherine de Medicis, [30] 4) Ronsard's own reiterated avowals of faith should not be gainsaid, [31] and 5) although Ronsard's flesh was

---

[30] For the history and consequences of this poem and the rest of the polemics, see, in addition to Dupré, Perdrizet, Charbonnier, and Chamard, E. J. Dubedout's "Les Discours de Ronsard," *MP,* I (1903-1904), 437-456, emphasizing Ronsard's sincerity. See, also, Jean Baillou's objective account in his edition of the *Discours des Misères de ce Temps* (Paris, 1949). As an indication of the court's reaction and that of Ronsard's adversaries, Dupré cites (pp. 557-558) Colletet's well-known, if not entirely accurate, account of the public thanks bestowed upon Ronsard by the *régente,* the king, and Pious V as well as of the calumnious counterattack of "ceux de la religion réformée," which had for its effect to "aiguiser son esprit et sa colère, de telle façon que luy, qui s'estoit tousjours si à propos aydé des lettres profanes, sçeut si bien, pour la deffense de l'Eglise et du sien propre, apporter les thrésors et les richesses de l'Egypte en la Terre saincte, que l'on recogneut incontinent que toute l'élégance et toute la douceur des lettres humaines et sacrées n'estoint pas du costé des hérétiques, comme ils le prétendoient." Laumonier in his edition of Claude Binet's *La Vie de Ronsard* (Paris, 1909), p. 152, notes that the papal felicitations, also reported by Binet, were never published and seriously questions the biographer's reliability on this point.

[31] For example, we read in his *Epistre au Lecteur* (1563): "Quand j'ai voulu escrire de Dieu, encore que la langue d'homme ne soit suffisante ny capable de parler de sa Majesté, je l'ai fait toutesfois le mieux qu'il m'a esté possible.... Moi, pauvre, infirme et humilié, je me confesse indigne de la recherche de ses secrets et du tout vaincu de la puissance de sa déité, obéissant à l'Eglise catholique, sans estre si ambitieux rechercheur de ces nouveautez qui n'apportent nulle seureté de conscience, comme rappelant toujours en doute les principaux poincts de nostre religion, lesquels il faut croire fermement et non curieusement en disputer" (*Œuvres,* Buon, 1623, II, 1616. Cited by Dupré, pp. 558-559). The fideism of this passage is self-evident. Henri Weber (*Création,* pp. 49-52) deals with the problem of "Fidéisme et Scepticisme" in Ronsard and after commenting on the well-known passages from the *Epitafe de Jan Martin,* the *Elégie à Robert de la Haye,* and the *Remonstrance* (V, 256-257; X, 321; XI, 71) concludes finally in favor of Ronsard's sincerity as against the suggestion of a subversive fideism leading to scepticisme: "Il n'est pas sûr que cette séparation de la raison et de la

undeniably weak, his spirit was willing. [32] Laumonier notes, however, that it took a certain amount of courage on Ronsard's part to supplicate Catherine, who at the time was leaning away from the Guises, to have the prince, Charles IX, instructed in the faith of his fathers and to "appaiser ce mechef" (XI, 21, n. 4):

> Il faut donq' des jeunesse instruire bien un prince
> Afin qu'aveq prudence il tienne sa province.
> Il faut premierement qu'il ait devant les yeux
> La crainte d'un seul Dieu: qu'il soit devotieux
> Envers la sainte Eglise, & que point il ne change
> La foy de ses ayeulz pour en prendre une estrange.
>
> (XI, 20-21)

There is, it appears little point in denying, in most cases, the accent of sincerity and the reasonableness of his conservative and orthodox views expressed in the various *Discours*. The pictures he paints, for example, of the dissension, disorder, sacrilege, and violence growing greater with each passing day are characteristically conservative as are the verses in which, describing the innovators, the poet, "logicien impitoyable les met en opposition avec eux-mêmes" (Dupré, p. 564):

> Et quoy! bruler maisons, piller & brigander,
> Tuer, assassiner, par force commander,
> N'obeir plus aux Roys, amasser des armées,
> Appellez vous cela Eglises reformées?
> JESUS, que seulement vous confessez icy
> De bouche & non de cœur, ne faisoit pas ainsi :
> Et S. Paul en preschant n'avoit pour toutes armes
> Sinon l'humilité, les jeusnes & les larmes,
> Et les Peres Martyrs, aux plus dures saisons
> Des Tyrans, ne s'armoyent sinon que d'oraisons,
> Bien qu'un Ange du ciel à leur moindre priere

---

foi soit toujours au bénéfice de la religion. Les tempéraments épicuriens, comme Ronsard, y trouvent une distinction commode, réservant le domaine de la foi comme indiscutable et inaccessible, ils s'abandonnent d'autant plus facilement aux caprices de leur imagination panthéiste, à leurs rêves mythologiques et païens. Si chez Ronsard la foi paraît, malgré tout, sincère, le fidéisme peut n'être chez d'autres qu'un paravent commode de l'incrédulité" (p. 52).

[32] Or as Dupré puts it: "S'il n'a pas eu la force de les [ses principes] mettre en pratique, il avait au moins, le courage de les affirmer, quand l'occasion s'en présentait" (p. 559).

En souflant eust rué les Tyrans en arriere.
"Mais par force on ne peult Paradis violer:
JESUS nous a monstré le chemin d'y aller:
Armez de patience il faut suyvre sa voye,
Celuy qui ne la suit se damne & se forvoye.

(*Continuation du Discours*, XI, 37-38) [33]

---

[33] Since Dupré's study rarely, if ever, is cited in discussions of Ronsard's Christianity, is of difficult access, and since many of his observations remain valid, it is necessary to resume, as briefly as possible, the principal bases of his apology of Ronsard's religion. He is quick to savor Ronsard's evocation of the "Christ empistollé" (*Continuation du Discours*, XI, 42) symbolizing the contradiction of the Huguenot outrage; cites the oft-quoted credo (*Responce aux injures*, XI, 135 ff.), of which Charbonnier aptly remarks: "C'est une paraphrase fort exacte du *Credo* catholique, et les beaux vers y abondent: Ronsard, si médiocre dans les œuvres exclusivement religieuses... excelle à démontrer sa foi quand elle est attaquée" (*Poésie française*, p. 390); adduces among other familiar passages Ronsard's refutation of the charge of atheism: "Apellés vous Athée un homme qui deteste..." (*Continuation du Discours*, XI, 45) as well as his affirmation of the divine right of kings: "Or, Sire, pour autant que nul n'a le pouvoir / De chastier les Roys..." (*Institution pour l'adolescence*, XI, 12), stressing throughout the poet's political and religious conservatism. Dupré also quotes copiously from the *Remonstrance*, the *Responce*, the *Prière à Dieu pour la Victoire*: "Donne, Seigneur, que nostre ennemy vienne" (XI, 63-106; 116-176; XVII.3, 401-408), from the 'religious' *Hinne à Saint Gervaise, et Protaise* (II, 5-7) and also mentions *Des pères de famille à Monsieur S. Blaise*: "Sainct Blaise, qui vis aux Cieux..." (*Œuvres complètes de Ronsard*, ed. Hugues Vaganay, Paris, 1924, VI, 246-250), the *Epitaphe de Louise de Mailly*, and two sonnets from the *Derniers Vers*. In addition Dupré shows the awkwardness of the Reformers' accusations of errors in the Church while at the same time protesting their own exclusive claim to revealed truth. The orthodoxy and constancy of the Guises, "devenus le plus ferme espoir des vrais catholiques" (p. 571), are evoked as well as the spectre conjured up by Ronsard of a divided France ravaged from within (*Elégie à Guillaume des Autels*, X, 357). The *Remonstrance*, "une charge à fond contre les hérétiques et un abbatis énorme de leurs sophismes les plus spécieux," is employed especially to illustrate what Dupré believes Ronsard "croit d'esprit et de cœur" (p. 571):

>Mais l'Evangile sainct du Sauveur Jesuschrist,
>M'a fermement gravée une foy dans l'esprit,
>Que je ne veux changer pour une autre nouvelle,
>Et deussai-je endurer une mort trescruelle.
> De tant de nouveautez je ne suis curieux:
>Il me plaist d'imiter le train de mes ayeux...
>
>   (XI, 67)

Dupré notes that Ronsard in the same poem not only continues to elaborate on the famous myth of *Opinion*, "fille de l'erreur," but, also, frankly admits and describes the "maux invétérés de l'Eglise" (p. 572). Thus Ronsard, "juge et partie dans la question... plaide contre ses propres intérêts, au risque

In the foregoing recapitulation of Dupré's apologia of Ronsard's Christianity not only has due credit been given to a neglected critic but also it has been shown that 1) the substantial body of poems and passages adduced, by its physical dimensions alone, quickly convinces us that the material comprises a significant part of Ronsard's total production, 2) that it is more pervasive than is commonly held [34] and 3) the tendency persists to color our appreciation of Ronsard's poetry by the notion we have of his sycophantic bent and by the consideration of other factors which may obscure rather than illuminate the aesthetic and philosophical interplay between his conflicting Humanism and Christianity. To say the least, it is impossible to ignore justifiably the coloration imparted by the former to the latter, even if we accept the hypothesis that Ronsard ultimately departs significantly from the Christian view of man. [35]

To sum up, then, the image of Ronsard, the Christian poet, may not, perhaps, so easily be discarded by reference to his expediency

---

de s'accuser le premier. L'irrégularité de sa position personnelle venait à l'appui de ses critiques générales; c'était un exemple, entre mille, de l'abus qu'il avait le courage et la loyauté de signaler" (p. 573). As for the *Responce*, the nineteenth-century critic chooses to emphasize the Christian orthodoxy of passages like the credo in which Ronsard opposes to the "false" and "odious" accusation of atheism "une affirmation nette et précise des vérités fondamentales du christianisme" (p. 576.) For the rest, although our apologist admits that the "suite ne répondit pas toujours à ces commencements admirables" (p. 577), we are treated to such verses as those depicting the poet's piously begun and ended day, with lines like "J'ayme à faire l'amour... (vv. 551-554) carefully omitted (*Responce*, XI, 144-145). Nor is the prosopopoeia of Louis XI forgotten, in which he wrathfully laments the Huguenots' depredation of his beloved church at Cléry. With a final quote from the epitaph to Louise de Mailly, Dupré concludes: "Voilà, sans doute, plus de citations qu'il n'en fallait pour établir que Ronsard, loin d'être hostile aux idées religieuses, leur prêtait volontiers l'appui de son talent poétique; heureux s'il eût toujours conformé ses mœurs et ses actes à une règle aussi pure! Etrange contradiction du cœur de l'homme, qui *approuve le meilleur et fait le pire*, suivant la remarque éternellement applicable d'un poète païen: *Video meliora proboque, deteriora sequor!*" (p. 582). Curiously enough, Dupré, although he appears to accept the polemic poetry at close to face value, almost completely ignores the philosophical poetry despite the numerous passages that they contain bearing on the nature of God, man, and the soul.

[34] This fact is even more impressive when viewed in the light of Dupré's almost total neglect of the *Hymnes* of 1555-1556.

[35] Much of the *Derniers Vers*, the *Fragment d'un poème de la loy divine*, and even "Les Hymnes sont des grecs invention première..." would seem alone to invalidate such an hypothesis.

and conservatism. To view his Christianity as fortuitous or grossly self-serving is less satisfactory than to attempt to see it as an integral part serving to illuminate the whole. Apologists like Dupré become all too easy marks for the researcher and logician intent upon establishing Ronsard's basic divorce from the faith of his fathers. This is a cause for regret, for in our haste to discover the 'real' Ronsard, as revealed through certain fundamental philosophical attitudes, we run the risk of losing sight of the poet grappling with the problem of the duality of man's condition. The epitaph to Louise de Mailly is "touchante" (Dupré, p. 582) because of this struggle in which the contradictory elements of Ronsard's longing for spiritual and earthly totality become the very stuff of the creative act. The nature of the Christian element's contribution to the epitaph can be understood best as a fusion of the real and the imagined worlds into a new poetic reality — a reality that would be quite different without the poet's conscious use of his Christian heritage.

The works of Ronsard showing an important Christian influence may be grouped for purposes of convenience, without violating logic, into four main blocks: 1) occasional verse having various political, personal, or ceremonial inspirations and comprising poems of a purely perfunctory Christian cast like the *Avantentrée du Roi treschrestien à Paris* (1549) as well as others in which the Christian element is a major aesthetic factor, 2) almost all of the philosophical *Hymnes* of 1555-1556, 3) the polemic poetry, i.e., the *Discours* and related pieces, and 4) the purely religious poems such as the *Hymne des Pères de Famille à Saint Blaise*. From these general categories and from the *Derniers Vers* it is feasible at present to consider only an arbitrary selection as a means of characterizing the nature of Ronsard's Christian inspiration in a preliminary way and of presenting some of the major critical stances taken on the problem.

From the *Hymnes*, written relatively early, the following poems seem to have prompted somewhat more interest than the others: *Hymne de la Justice, Le Temple du Connestable et des Chastillons, Hymne de la Philosophie, Prière à la Fortune, Les Daimons, Hymne du Ciel, Hymne des Astres, Hymne de la Mort, Hercule Chrestien,* and *Hymne de l'Eternité*.[36] The *Hymne de la Philosophie,*

---

[36] In passing it should be noted that the Ronsardian *Hymne* defies ready classification. For a review of the question and a new proposed definition

which is of crucial importance for the understanding of Ronsard's ultimate philosophy, contains a substantial Christian element.[37] The poem, which has been grouped with the *Prière à la Fortune* and the *Hercule Chrestien* by virtue of the fact that it is written in decasyllabics and dedicated to Cardinal de Chastillon,[38] has other more significant points in common with these two poems and the other *Hymnes*, whatever arbitrarily established category they may fall into: heroic, didactic, mythological, philosophical, lyric, epic, or religious. Instead of separating in our minds the inspiration, both philosophical and poetic, of the *Hercule Chrestien,* for example, from that of the *Hymne de la Philosophie* and the other philosophical poems, we have in all likelihood something to gain from examining some of the poems in the light of the others. Certainly not only the recurrence of themes but also the very architecture of the collection invites us to do so.[39]

Ronsard in the *Hymne de la Philosophie* views philosophy as encompassing all areas of human interest, the *lettres* as well as the *sciences.*[40] Theology, by the back door of demonology, enters the list, which includes cosmology, law, medicine, astrology, and even

---

of the genre, see Michel Dassonville's "Eléments pour une définition de l'Hymne Ronsardien," *BHR,* XXIV (1962), 58-76. After considering such "définitions insatisfaisantes" (p. 63) as Cohen's "l'inspiration des hymnes est en général politique, religieuse et philosophique" (*Ronsard,* p. 171), Dassonville remarks, significantly for us, that "le lyrisme s'affirme dans la plupart des hymnes par le sentiment religieux. Non pas qu'ils soient pleins de déclarations de principes ou de professions de foi, mais d'une religiosité sous-jacente, puissante, d'une émotion quasi-mystique en face des merveilles de l'Univers" (p. 75).

[37] Large enough, it seems, to give us pause once more before accepting Busson's relegation of the genuinely Christian Hymnes to the status of a passing stage in Ronsard's gradual evolution toward materialism.

[38] By Alice Klengel in her *Pierre de Ronsards Hymnendichtung* (Leipzig, 1931), p. 83. Such otiose groupings attest once again to a general confusion and misunderstanding as to the more profound poetic unity of the *Hymnes* of 1555-1556.

[39] For example, although Ronsard's corrections and suppressions in the successive editions of his works have received with great positive effect continuing critical attention, comparatively little has been said as to the importance of the retention of poems such as the *Hercule Chrestien* and the bulk of other 'Christian' passages in the *Hymnes.*

[40] See Laumonier's comment, *Œuvres,* VIII, 86, n. 2.

magic.[41] Early in this long poem Ronsard, after the customary genuflexion to his Muse — in this case Clio — and to the "grandeur" and "vertu" of Odet de Coligny, describes *Philosophie*, already personified and moving on a plane with the gods and angels, in the following fashion:

> Elle, voyant qu'à l'homme estoit nyé
> D'aller au Ciel, disposte, a delié
> Loing, hors du corps, nostre Ame emprisonnée,
> Et par esprit aux astres l'a menée,
> Car en dressant de nostre Ame les yeux,
> Haute, s'attache aux merveilles des Cieux,
> Vaguant par tout, & sans estre lassée
> Tout l'Univers discourt en sa pensée,
> Et seulle peut des astres s'alïer
> Osant de DIEU la nature espïer.
>
> (VIII, 86-87)[42]

Philosophy is seen, then, for all her power to encompass and comprehend the universe and to liberate man's mind from the heavy shackles of the body, as acting not without a certain presumption: "*Osant* de DIEU la nature espïer." In the hierarchy thereby implied it is patently absurd to separate Ronsard's philosophy from his theology. Given the substantive Christian passages of the other *Hymnes*, it is not without interest to note its presence here and how it is linked to poems like *Les Daimons*:

> Or' deux extremitez ne sont point sans meillieu,
> Et deux extremitez sont les hommes & DIEU.
> DIEU, qui est tout puissant, de nature eternelle,
> Les hommes, impuissans, de nature mortelle:
> Des hommes & de DIEU, les DAIMONS aërins
> Sont communs en nature, habitans les confins
> De la Terre & du Ciel, & dans l'air se delectent,

---

[41] See Laumonier, *loc. cit.*, and Busson who characterizes Ronsard's notion of philosophy as "rejoignant... la théologie qui en est cependant distincte" and as embracing "toutes les sciences" (*Rationalisme*, pp. 362-363, n. 2). The distinction being, one assumes, that theology differs from philosophy in that it attempts to deal with truths not accessible to reason alone.

[42] Ronsard habitually peoples his universe with pagan and Christian divinities and supernatural agents along with abstractions like *Philosophie* and *Clémence* as, for example, in the *Hymne de la Justice*: "Dieu transmist la JUSTICE en l'âge d'or ça bas..." (VIII, 50, vv. 49 ff.).

Et sont bons ou mauvais tout ainsi qu'ilz s'affectent.
Les bons viennent de l'air jusques en ces bas lieux,
Pour nous faire sçavoir la volonté des Dieux,
Puis r'emportent à DIEU noz faictz & nos prieres,
Et detachent du corps noz ames prisonnieres
Pour les mener là-haut, à fin d'imaginer
Ce qui se doit sçavoir pour nous endoctriner.

(VIII, 125-126)

Whether the intermediary be Philosophy or Demon, we find in Ronsard no subtle — or artificial — dividing line between the provinces of theology, of superstition, or of rational intellection. In the passage from *Philosophie* it is clearly Philosophy that holds the promise of ultimate knowledge and yet in the concluding verse it is evidently a question of theology, the science of religion, of the Divine. So, too, are the Demons relegated to a subordinate role as instruments for the apprehension of Divine knowledge and will. The question, however, is not so much whether theology preoccupies Ronsard but, rather, what form does it assume. Is it Christian or 'Pagan'? Here is what we read in the hymn to Philosophy:

Elle congnoist des Anges les essences,
Leur hierarchie, & toutes les puissances
Des grands Daimons, & des Herôs, plus bas
Que les Daimons, le siege & les estats,
Et comme DIEU, par eux nous admonneste,
Et comme promptz ilz portent la requeste
De l'homme au Ciel, eux habitans le lieu
De l'air, qui est des hommes & de DIEU
Egual-distant, & comme tous les songes
Se font par eux vrais, ou plains de mensonges,
Car elle sçait les bons & les mauvais,
Leurs qualitez, leur forme, & leurs effectz,
Et leur mystere, & ce qu'on leur doit faire
Pour les facher, ou bien pour leur complaire :
Et pourquoy c'est qu'ilz sont tant desireux
De la matiere, & couhards, & poureux,
Craignant le coup d'une tranchante espée,
Et par quel art leur nature est trompée
Des enchanteurs, qui les tiennent serrez
Estroitement dans des anneaux ferrez,
Ensorcelez, ou par une figure,
Ou par le bruit d'un magique murmure,

D'espritz divins se rendans serviteurs
(Tant ilz sont sotz) des humains enchanteurs.
(VIII, 87-89)

The passage is interesting for at least two reasons. First, in it we find a characteristic mélange of Christian, popular, and pagan religious terminology: the specifically Christian angels together with Demons commingled with pagan Heroes, each taking an assigned place in a hierarchy dominated by the sublime *DIEU*. Second, these lines are representative of those, frequent in Ronsard, which on the surface appear to indicate on his part not only a juggling of incompatible systems and traditions but, also, a mental confusion resulting in poetry that has been the despair of those seeking a coherent vision of the universe in Ronsard's total works. The world view now emerging, however, from the juxtaposition of seemingly incommensurable elements is, upon closer examination, found not wanting in cohesion and clarity. Quite to the contrary, we may note in these passages the rigorous separation of function and domain for each category of beings. The impression made upon us is one of control and vigorous mastery in organization and presentation. The poet orders apparently disproportionate ideas and from them creates an image of great stability. This feeling in the main is communicated by the strong and forcefully articulated syntax: the emphatic inversion of *des anges les essences,* the unusual relief imparted to possessives and the uncompromising qualifiers: "*leur* hierarchie ... *toutes* les puissances," and so on. Our attention is brought to bear on the careful conjunction of the separate parts and at the same time the subject of the poem is invested with the qualities of the manner of presentation. [43]

The same vigor of presentation is carried over to the description of the essential qualities of the Demons. Thus, Ronsard, quite like the schoolmen, brings logical disputation to bear on intrinsic mysteries and there is no compelling reason for considering

---

[43] On Ronsard's cosmology, see Isidore Silver's "Ronsard's Reflections on Cosmology and Nature," *PMLA,* LXXIX (June 1964), 219-233, in which Ronsard is described as "in his later years inclined toward a denial of creation" (p. 226) and his declining years as characterized by a "mood of resigned acquiescence to natural law" (p. 233).

Ronsard's DIEU as any other than the Christian God.[44] Indeed, later on it is clear that Ronsard, even as he extolls "mighty" Philosophy, takes care not to allow her dominion to surpass or even encroach upon the supreme Deity's, for her power's ultimate limit is, significantly enough, represented by the conquest of the pagan *Dieux* and their sovereign Jupiter:

> Donc, à bon droit cette PHILOSOPHIE
> D'un Jupiter les menaces defie,
> Qui plein d'orgueil, se vante que les Dieux
> Ne le sçauroient à bas tirer des Cieux,
> Tirassent ilz d'une main conjurée
> Le bout pendant de la cheine ferrée,
> Et que luy seul, quand bon luy semblera,
> Tous de sa cheîne au Ciel les tirera.
> Mais les effors d'une telle science
> Tire les Dieux, & la mesme puissance
> De Jupiter, & comme tous charmez
> Dedans du bois les detient enfermez.
>
> (VIII, 89-90) [45]

---

[44] The capitalized form is not adventitious in the *Hymnes*. A look at its appearance in the collection shows that it is to be distinguished from both *Dieu* and *dieu(x)*.

[45] See Laumonier, VIII, 90, n. 2: "Cette chaîne, dit Richelet, 'n'est rien autre chose que l'ordre, la raison et la suitte des causes et choses créées, qui dépend de la puissance et volonté de Dieu.'" Somewhat in the same vein are verses 259-272, which not only state again Philosophy's ascendancy over the forces that are represented by the pagan divinities but also clearly show that their figurative value is uppermost in Ronsard's mind. Passages like this run counter to the opinion that Ronsard was naïvely superstitious or that his use of mythology was superficial and puerile:

> Qu'esse le Roc promené de Sisyphe,
> Et les pommons empietez de la griffe
> Du grand Vautour? & qu'esse le Rocher
> Qui fait semblant de vouloir trebucher
> Sur Phlegias? & la Roüe meurdriere?
> Et de Tantal' la soif en la riviere?
> "Si non le soing qui jamais ne s'enfuit
> "De nostre cœur...
> ... ...
> Mais toy [Chastillon], qui as hors de ton cœur bien loing
> Tousjours chassé ce miserable soing,
> Tu as gaigné le haut de la Montaigne,
> D'où ta pitié maintenant nous enseigne,
> Ainsi que toy, d'ensuyvre la Vertu,
> Non par le trac du grand chemin batu
> Du peuple sot, ains par l'estroite voye
> Qui l'homme sage à la Vertu convoye.
>
> (VIII, 100)

Philosophy also has intimate knowledge of God's creation and of its harmonious mechanism, having learned "comment tout le firmament dance, / Et comme DIEU le guide à la cadance" (VIII, 91), but there is no hint as to her final ascendancy.[46]

Philosophy's function, if well-defined, is nonetheless broad: to teach man to apprehend the God, flee Evil, and be constant of heart ("douter de rien"), vv. 105-106; still, although the following description of Hell is thoroughly pagan (vv. 107-125), the last retreat selected by Philosophy, now Virtue, after the enlightenment, "sur le haut d'un Rocher" (v. 190), corresponds, as Laumonier points out, "à l'enseignement traditionnel de la scolastique" (VIII, 97, n. 1).[47] In addition, Ronsard explains that the pagan Hell as he describes it is intended as the figurative representation of man's own self-fashioned Hell on earth. We may conclude, then, that in the mixture of pagan and Christian elements the poet appears to be no less orthodox in his expression than the medieval schoolmen intent on reconciling the two traditions. He attempts, however, no purely rational explanation of the great mysteries of life. The poem is, above all, a lesson — stoic, it is true — in how to live both lucidly and virtuously:

> Je te salue ô grand PHILOSOPHIE:
> Quiconque soit cettuy-là qui se fie
> En tes propos, d'un courage constant,
> Vivra tousjours bien-heureux & content,
> Sans craindre rien, comme celuy qui pense
> Que de nul mal la Vertu ne s'offence.
>
> (VIII, 102)

It may be argued, of course, that Ronsard would be disinclined to go far in the direction of scepticism in a poem dedicated to the "reverendissime" Cardinal de Chastillon and that the Christian element is hardly essential to Ronsard's admonition to live wisely and well. Nowhere, however, does Philosophy, whose mission is to

---

[46] In this respect the *Hymne de la Philosophie* might be adduced as further evidence in support of Ronsard's authentic fideism with a positive scepticism as its basis.

[47] In the same note Laumonier also points out that the suppression of the passage in 1584 was due in all likelihood to a desire to present *Vertu* in not so harsh surroundings.

preserve us from "un trop engourdy somme" (v. 183), invite us to challenge faith and theology on the basis of reason and science, nor do we find a hint of such a suggestion in the poem. [48]

If the Christian element in the *Hymne de la Philosophie*, for all of that, is relatively slight and for the most part conventional — even in the reconciliation of divergent traditions — such is hardly the case in *Les Daimons*. The poem is replete with Christian terms, images, and themes. It is of further significance in its attempted fusion of Humanism and Christianity in a way that is much more complex than in the *Hymne de la Philosophie*. At the same time the poem promises to be more revealing and characteristic of Ronsard's religious thought and, most important, of his method of poetic reconciliation of apparent theological or philosophical opposites. Commentary on the poem is, therefore, representative of much of the critical debate concerning the fundamental quality of Ronsard's religious and philosophical poetry. Gustave Cohen regards the poem as presenting an "ambigu de paganisme," de folklore et du christianisme du plus curieux effet" and concludes generally against the importance of the Christian element in Ronsard (see *supra*, n. 10). There is in corroboration and in opposition to this point of view a considerable amount of critical opinion. Charbonnier, for example, looks upon *Les Daimons* as a wholly puerile and censurable example of superstitious credulousness and shallow religiosity (*La poésie française et les guerres de Religion*, pp. 452-454). Franchet (*Le poète et son œuvre*, pp. 251-252) includes the poem in his discussion of Ronsard's alleged superstitious beliefs and pictures the poet as credulously indulging his taste for such "diableries" as depicted in the famous passage describing his routing of the Demons which had beset him by night (VIII, 134-135). [49]

The views of both Cohen and Franchet well illustrate how insensitivity to the aesthetic importance of Ronsard's Christian inspiration results in the rejection of a good deal of evidence indicating a less naïve fusion of disparate elements than either critic seems

---

[48] Chamard remarks that philosophical science for Ronsard is "ni une psychologie ni une théologie; c'est une cosmologie" (*Histoire*, II, 186) or "science de l'univers" (p. 186).

[49] Despite the suppression of the passage in 1584 and 1587.

to be willing to concede. Henri Weber, on the other hand, citing verses 59-64, looks upon the poem as, among other things, conciliating "l'animisme qui préside à la mythologie antique, et la religion chrétienne: les nymphes, les naïades et les divinités payennes devenant des démons" (*Création,* p. 44), yet does not discount the hair-raising reality of the "terreurs superstitieuses que ressentait parfois Ronsard, comme en témoigne l'*Hymne des Démons*" (p. 497). Even more important, Weber in his appraisal of the poetic merit of the poem devotes a long essay to "La fusion du sentiment panthéiste avec la poésie des croyances populaires" (pp. 515-522). Curiously enough, however, Weber, who of all of the critics who have concerned themselves with the problem of Ronsard's Christianity most consistently points to an aesthetic approach for the solution of the problem and who is most aware of the "sentiment puissant de la fécondité et de l'unité de la vie, qui circule à travers les plus intimes parties de l'univers" of Ronsard (p. 521), is unable, or unwilling, in respect to the philosophical poetry to go beyond the affirmation that the "christianisme de l'auteur n'y ajoute qu'exceptionellement une vibration plus pathétique" (p. 522). Henri Chamard, also, is only partially satisfying as he dwells on the curious and strange "matière" (*Histoire,* II, 190) of the poem, characterizing it as "tout rempli de superstitions populaires" (II, 190) and as "pseudo-scientifique" (II, 189). A. Müller (*La poésie religieuse,* p. 153, n. 5) excludes the poem from his consideration of a poet who "faisait preuve d'une loyauté indiscutable, d'une sincérité émouvante dans sa manière de traduire les inquiétudes de l'homme devant les mystères qui entourent son berceau et sa tombe. Comment à ce titre ne méritait-il pas d'être cité ici?" (p. 153). A. M. Schmidt,[50] whose studies figure most prominently in respect to *Les Daimons,* has shown a considerable and variable Christian element in the poem. It is present in a variety of important ways ranging from the question of Ronsard and Saint Thomas on the nature of angels (pp. 16, 28, 45 *et passim*) — Schmidt stating at one point that the "angélologie de Ronsard ... ne diffère pas sensiblement de celle que le thomisme constitua" (p. 16) — to the questions of Ronsard as an

---

[50] See his critical edition of *Pierre de Ronsard: Hymne des Daimons* (Paris, 1939).

imitator of biblical writers, his relationship to the church Fathers, the schoolmen (pp. 23-26), Ronsard and the Fathers on the question of the birth of Demons (pp. 36-37), the Neoplatonic element in Ronsard's Christianity (p. 42), the cautious conclusion of the *Hymne* revealing an "accent véritablement chrétien" (p. 74), and, finally, the history of the successive variants explained by reference to Ronsard's desire to suppress features "capables de blesser la sensibilité religieuse de ses contemporains" and to his "sentiment très fin de la décence chrétienne" (p. 76). All of these factors in addition to the continuing attempt to fuse the two traditions — evident both in the text and in almost every other line of the recondite, complex commentary provided by Schmidt — serve to emphasize the importance and relevance of the Christian influence in the poem. [51]

Albert-Marie Schmidt notwithstanding [52] and limiting ourselves to what may well be the predominant *raison d'être* of the *Hymne des Daimons* — namely, the conscious attempt to unite Christian with pagan and popular beliefs — the following observations may be made: 1) The poem is, of course, significantly theological:

> ... il est temps que j'envoye
> Ma Muse dedans l'air par une estroicte voye,
> Qui de noz peres mortz aux vieux temps ne fut pas
> (Tant elle est incongneüe) empreinte de leurs pas,
> Afin d'estre promeüe au mystere admirable
> Des DAIMONS ...
>
> (VIII, 118)

---

[51] It is difficult to accept Schmidt's conclusion suggesting a kind of arcane message intended only for the initiate: "Enfin, si à partir de 1584, il sacrifie à ses scrupules le récit, peut-être paré, de sa lutte contre les Daimons (vers 347-378), c'est vraisemblablement que, champion de la cause catholique, il ne veut pas se découvrir devant ses adversaires et accréditer un fâcheux renom de possédé qui eût pu faire de lui un compagnon malfamé des Agrippa et des Paracelse. D'ailleurs le bon du conte provient de sa délicate astuce: il biffe la narration un peu trop caractéristique de la chasse sauvage à laquelle il se laissa entaîner, mais épargne les vers où, de façon abstraite, il mentionne ses passes d'arme nocturnes contre les mauvais esprits: il n'en faut pas plus pour que les habiles soient avertis de ses véritables manières. Ainsi, tout au cours de son œuvre, Ronsard, parlant à des initiés, tend à dissimuler, ou du moins à atténuer par un sobre contexte ses intuitions magiques fondamentales: il charge le poète de masquer le mage. Il y parvient si bien que l'opinion littéraire moyenne de nos jours considérerait volontiers comme délirante toute tentative de faire tomber ce masque" (pp. 76-77).

[52] See n. 51.

2) The cosmology is expressed in essentially hierarchic terms:

> Quand l'ETERNEL bastit la grand'maison du monde,
> Il peupla de poissons les abysmes de l'Onde,
> D'hommes la Terre, & l'air de Daimons, & les Cieux
> D'Anges, à celle-fin qu'il n'y eut point de lieux
> Vagues dans l'Univers, &, selon leurs natures,
> Qu'ilz fussent tous remplys de propres creatures.
> Il meit aupres de luy (car ainsi le voulut)
> L'escadron precieux des Anges, qu'il eleut
> Pour citoyens du Ciel, qui sans corps y demeurent,
> Et, francz de passions, non plus que luy ne meurent:
> Car ilz ne sont qu'Espris divins, parfaictz & purs,
> Qui congnoissent les ans tant passez, que futurs,
> Et tout estat mondain, comme voyant les choses
> De pres, au seing de DIEV, où elles sont encloses.
>
> (VIII, 119)

3) It is by the will of God ("par le vouloir de DIEU," v. 82) that the Demons inhabit the sublunar zone lower than the angels, the "espris divins" (vv. 69-72), and higher than the earthly mortals. Interestingly enough, these beings, likened by Ronsard to the "exercite des nües" (v. 83), are in their characteristic suppleness and constant process of transformation presented not as agents of disorder, chaos, or magical powers but as elements of a well-ordered universe made up of closely articulated parts. Their manifold transformations, for all the extraordinary diversity of forms, are subject, like the clouds, to restrictions of space and substance. The effect, as in the *Hymne de la Philosophie* (*supra,* pp. 38-40) and amid all the movement and change, is, still, one of a certain order:

> Ne plus ne moins qu'on voit l'exercite des nües,
> En un temps orageux egalement pendües
> D'un juste poix en l'air, marcher ainsi qu'il faut,
> Ny descendant trop bas, ny s'eslevant trop haut:
> Et tout ainsi qu'on voit qu'elles mesmes se forment
> En cent diversitez, dont les vents les transforment
> En Centaures, Serpens, Oiseaux, Hommes, Poissons,
> Et d'une forme en l'autre errent en cent façons:
> Tout ainsi les DAIMONS ...
>
> (VIII, 120) [53]

---

[53] These lines appear to be contradicted by vv. 114-115, in which the Demons are described as taking on their form and color by their own

4) The Demons, who have dominion over us by their hold on the imagination, vv. 125-132, are also intermediary metaphysical entities:

> Ilz sont participants de DIEU, & des humains:
> De DIEU, comme immortelz, & de nous, comme pleins
> De toutes passions: ilz desirent, ilz craignent,
> Ilz veulent conçevoir, ilz ayment & dedaignent,
> Et n'ont rien propre à eux que le corps seulement
> Faict d'air, corps non commun à DIEU totalement:
> Car DIEU n'est qu'unité, & qu'une simple essence,
> Et les corps des humains de terre ont pris naissance.
>
> (VIII, 123)

5) Much of the significance of verses 201-208 ff. [54] is obscured by Schmidt's judgment that Ronsard is merely being careful to "conserver dans sa démonologie certains rudiments de christianisme" (p. 42), for not only do the Demons act as the gods' agents but they also carry our prayers back to *DIEU* and liberate our souls to apprehend what is essential for our instruction (vv. 212-214). [55] 6) The

---

"action" and "volonté" yet, significantly enough, in a perfectly natural and not at all sinister way: like the paling or reddening of one's face in response to fear or shame (vv. 115-118).

[54] See supra, pp. 37-38.

[55] "Et detachent du corps noz ames prisonnieres / Pour les mener là-haut, à fin d'imaginer / Ce qui se doit sçavoir pour nous endoctriner" (VIII, 126). Three major points may be made in respect to these lines: 1) In them Ronsard views man's nature as specifically dualistic (the soul is prisoner of the body) and man in his disembodied form, like the Demons, may ascend "là-haut." The passage, then, has an important bearing on the question of Ronsard's notion of the relationship between the soul and the body. 2) The verses may not be viewed as any less genuine than those reflecting the occult science and the extraordinary fantasy of popular superstition expressed in the poem. Indeed, as we have seen, Ronsard suppressed in later editions the most farfetched episode: the poet's personal encounter with the Demons. 3) It is obvious from Ronsard's juxtaposition in these and preceding verses of the Christian Divinity and of *Dieux* acting as agents (like Demons) as well as from the clearly stated duality of man's nature that the poet is inviting us to consider his *Démons* and *Dieux* on a somewhat more lofty plane than the literal or superstitious. One may also recall in this respect verses 279-282 in which Demons are the motive powers of great natural forces: the tides, storms, and so on. Neptune, for example, is presented to us as but yet another Demon (v. 283). Henri Weber's remarks on "Le prestige du Mythe et la théorie de la vérité cachée" (*Création poétique*, pp. 132-134) illuminate Ronsard's characteristic use of figurative language. Of the *Hercule*

passage describing the various physical forms assumed by mischievous Demons (vv. 331-346), like the episode which follows it in which Ronsard tells of warding them off with his sword, should be regarded as pure fantasy. Ronsard says that they are illusory in nature, never appearing to men of understanding but, rather, to the easily abused and weak of heart:

> Que diray plus? ilz sont plains d'arts & de science,
> Quant au reste, impudens, & plains d'outrecuidance,
> Sans aucun jugement, ilz sont folletz, menteurs
> Volages, inconstans, traistres, & decepteurs,
> Mutins, impaciens, qui jamais n'apparoissent
> A ceux qui leur nature, & leurs abus congnoissent:
> Mais s'ilz voyent quelcun abandonné d'espoir,
> Errer seul dans un bois, le viendront deçevoir,
> Ou tromperont les cœurs des simplettes bergeres
> Qui gardent les brebis, & les feront sorcieres.
>
> (VIII, 136)

Finally, the concluding verses of the poem represent the Demons as totally under the dominion of God. Ronsard beseeches his eternal Lord that the Demons be banished far from Christendom to inflict havoc upon the Turks or, closer to home, upon the heads of the detractors of his benefactor, Lancelot de Carle. Such subaltern divinities can hardly be regarded as architects of man's destiny. And, though they appear elsewhere in Ronsard's works, they are absent from the *Derniers Vers*.

The *Hymne du Ciel*, variously described as "toute scientifique" (Franchet, *Le poète et son œuvre*, p. 207) or as a piece of "poésie cosmique" with Platonic and Aristotelian coloration (Chamard, *Histoire*, II, 188), is in a larger, and more accurate sense an attempt to animate the universe with ideas and beings presented metaphorically. Their relationships with one another tend to reveal not a simplistic world view exclusive of others but, rather, one essaying,

---

Chrestien, for example, he states: "Ronsard explique toujours très clairement le sens moral d'un mythe, sans se contenter de le suggérer par quelques indices qui ne seraient accessibles qu'à un petit nombre d'esprits éclairés. Il a procédé avec cette clarté dans l'*Hercule chrétien*, en cherchant à établir, suivant un procédé tout médiéval, une correspondance minutieuse entre chacun des travaux et certains épisodes de la vie du Christ" (p. 133).

it seems, an amalgamation of scientific, philosophical, and metaphysical ideas inspired ultimately by a profound religious sense and unified apprehension of the universe.[56] Thus, it is not through chance nor lack of consistency of vision that in the *Hymne du Ciel,* for all of its Platonic and Aristotelian content, we find the Christian idea of the *Ciel* as being the dwelling place of the Lord: "O Ciel net, pur, & beau, haute maison de DIEU" (v. 15); and we note the "idées chrétiennes"[57] of the following passage describing how the beauty and harmony of the firmament:

> Nous monstrent, en voyant un si bel edifice,
> Combien l'Esprit de DIEU est remply d'artifice,
> Et subtil artisan, qui te bastît de rien,
> Et t'acomplît si beau, pour nous monstrer combien
> Grande est ta Majesté, qui hautaine demande
> Pour son palais royal une maison si grande.
> Or' ce DIEU tout-puissant, tant il est bon, & doux,
> S'est faict le citoyen du Monde, comme nous,
> Et n'a tant dedaigné nostre humaine nature,
> Qu'il ait outre les bordz de ta large closture
> Autre maison bastie, ains s'est logé chez toy,
> Chez toy, franc de soucis, de peines, & d'esmoy,
> Qui vont couvrant le front des terres habitables,
> Des terres, la maison des humains miserables.
>
> (VIII, 145-146)

The *Hymne de la Mort* is of paramount importance for the question of Ronsard's orthodoxy, depth of conviction, and sincerity as to his overt expressions of Christian ideas.[58] For this reason the

---

[56] This poem has been looked upon as having a more apparent purely Christian element than the *Daimons* (Cohen, *Ronsard,* p. 176). Weber points out the important fact that it is more Christian than its major source, Marullus, would seem to indicate: "Sans parler de l'accent plus chrétien de Ronsard qui substitue le Dieu unique à la pluralité des divinités païennes..." (*Création poétique,* p. 485). He is careful, however, to emphasize, despite the Platonic and Christian elements, vv. 59-78, Ronsard's "conception de l'univers réduit à un beau jouet, à un mécanisme harmonieux, précis et sans mystère, dont Dieu est l'habile horloger" (p. 496).

[57] Lebègue, "Appendice," VIII, 370.

[58] Lebègue, though more aware of the necessity of accepting the genuineness of the Christian influence in the *Hymne* than was Laumonier in 1935, nevertheless notes, where Laumonier speaks of the "mélange de la foi chrétienne et des idées païennes chez Ronsard" (VIII, 172, n. 2), that it is perhaps more exact to specify a "mélange des dogmes chrétiens et des

reader's indulgence is asked for the reproduction of the following frequently cited passage:

> Tu me diras encor que tu trambles de crainte
> D'un batelier Charon, qui passe par contrainte
> Les ames outre l'eau d'un torrent effroyant,
> Et que tu crains le Chien à trois voix aboyant,
> Et les eaux de Tantal', & le roc de Sisyphe,
> Et des cruelles Sœurs & le fouet, & la griffe,
> Et tout cela qu'ont feint les poëtes là-bas
> Nous attendre aux Enfers apres nostre trespas.
>   Quiconques dis cecy, ha, pour Dieu! te souvienne
> Que ton ame n'est pas payenne, mais chrestienne,
> Et que nostre grant Maistre, en la Croix estendu
> Et mourant, de la MORT l'aiguillon a perdu,
> Et d'elle maintenant n'a faict qu'un beau passage
> A retourner au Ciel, pour nous donner courage
> De porter nostre croix, fardeau leger & doux,
> Et de mourir pour luy, comme il est mort pour nous,
> Sans craindre, comme enfans, la nacelle infernalle,
> Le rocher d'Ixion, & les eaux de Tantalle,
> Et Charon, & le chien Cerbere à trois abbois,
> Desquelz le sang de CHRIST t'afranchît en la Croix,
> Pourveu qu'en ton vivant tu luy veuilles complaire,
> Faisant ses mandemens qui sont aisez à faire:
> Car son joug est plaisant, gracieux & leger,
> Qui le dôs nous soulaige en lieu de le charger.
>   (VIII, 172)

In addition to the fact that the passage is far from standing alone in the poem as an expression of the Christian view of death (and life), we may note that once more [59] Ronsard has gone to some length to show explicitly the figurative use to which he puts his mythological and pagan material. It would be idle to repeat here the importance that the Christian element has in other passages of

---

mythes païens" (VIII, 372). Lebègue also points to themes in the *Hymne de la Mort* (vv. 138-139, 340-341) echoed some thirty years later in the *Derniers Vers* ("Appendice," pp. 371, 372). The first of these is of greater interest, for in it Christ is described as follows: "Qui vivant nous bailla ce chemin par escrit, / Et marqua de son sang ceste voye tressaincte, / Mourant tout le premier, pour nous oster la crainte" (VIII, 169, vv. 138-140).

[59] See n. 55.

the *Hymne de la Mort*.[60] Suffice it to say that, although much light has been cast upon Ronsard's dependence upon a variety of sources in the poem, opinion does not vary significantly in respect to the fact of the considerable part played by the Christian ideas expressed in it.[61] There is, however, little agreement as to how to assess the value of this element in respect to the poem's obvious eclecticism or syncretism. The disparity of the views expressed on this one poem is all the more intriguing in that it may be taken to represent not just a stage in the development of Ronsard's religious thought,[62] but, rather, as characteristic of the much more complex and crucial problem of the Christian element in the work of Ronsard taken as a whole.[63]

---

[60] For example, vv. 129-140, in which the reader is exorted to lead a life contrasting, in this instance, with Circe's swine: "Comme estans vrais enfans, & disciples de CHRIST" (VIII, 169).

[61] It is, nevertheless, well to note that Lebègue ("Appendice," pp. 370-372) shows an increased awareness of the importance of this presence. Even where Laumonier's notes make explicit reference to the Christian content, however, his preoccupations are clear as in the following remark on vv. 113-120: "Cette pensée toute chrétienne qu'elle paraisse, se trouve dans Plutarque..." (VIII, 168, n. 5). Cf. Lebègue's: "Le texte de Plutarque est bien différent..." (VIII, 371). Lebègue has been able to make some 9 corrections or additions to Laumonier's notes bearing on the Christian inspiration of the poem (VIII, 370-372).

[62] Cf. Hornik, "More on Ronsard's Philosophy," p. 443.

[63] Here, in addition to the studies already mentioned and in greatly abbreviated form, are some of the more representative positions taken upon the poem in recent years: Chamard, who is less than enthusiastic about Ronsard's use of Christian themes, acknowledges nonetheless, after sketching the complexity of the sources, that "ces sources bien indiquées, il faut reconnaître à Ronsard le mérite d'avoir su donner à son hymne une couleur toute chrétienne. Il y développe une idée essentiellement religieuse: c'est que la mort est bienfaisante, puisqu'elle nous délivre de la prison du corps, des misères de cette vie, des inconstances de la fortune, et qu'elle nous ouvre toutes grandes les portes de l'éternelle félicité" (*Histoire*, II, 202). Laumonier affirms that the *Hymne* "combine hardiment le plus pur christianisme et la doctrine d'Epicure" (*Ronsard poète lyrique*, p. 562). Weber notes what he calls its "facilité épicurienne" (*Création poétique*, p. 512) and characterizes the Christian element as being largely responsible for the beauty of vv. 319-336 "où le christianisme n'est plus juxtaposé artificiellement à la poésie antique mais en devient le complément, le déplacement lyrique" (p. 513). Hornik stresses the pervasive quality of its neoplatonism ("More on Ronsard's Philosophy"). Lebègue finds "dans l'*Hymne de la Mort*, si l'on écarte le fatras des imitations de l'Antiquité, ... un pathétique débat entre un Ronsard qui s'efforce de trouver dans la doctrine du Christ et dans la

The poems and passages in Ronsard's earlier writings illustrative of the fundamental importance of his use of the Christian inspiration have, as we have already suggested, significant echoes in his later work. So, too, of course, do the pagan attitudes towards the basic questions of immortality, the nature and fate of the soul, the birth and architecture of the universe, and so on. What concerns us here mainly, however, is that Ronsard returns so often, and more consistently than we may imagine, at different times during his life to a palpable Christian inspiration. His nostalgia for the religion of his forebears reveals itself not only explicitly in the philosophical, polemic, and ceremonial poetry, but also when the poet addresses himself to the ultimate questions in his moments of confrontation with the mysteries of life and death. Written at the end of his life, Ronsard's *Derniers Vers* constitute more than a melancholy declaration of his lassitude with life. They are, also, an overt acknowledgement of Christ as the redeemer and Savior:

> Quoy mon ame, dors tu engourdie en ta masse?
> La trompette a sonné, serre bagage, & va
> Le chemin deserté que Jesuchrist trouva,
> Quand tout mouillé de sang racheta nostre race.
>
> (XVIII, 179)

and:

> Il faut laisser maisons & vergers & Jardins,
> Vaisselles & vaisseaux que l'artisan burine,

---

sagesse antique des raisons de se résigner à la mort, et un autre Ronsard, qui fait sienne la célèbre boutade d'Achille (*Mieux vaut goujat debout qu'empereur enterré*, dira La Fontaine), qui a horreur de la décomposition des cadavres, et qui préfère à la décrépitude et à la maladie une mort soudaine" (*Ronsard*, p. 64). Müller devotes 3 pages to the *Hymne* and concludes in favor of a faith rarely "plus sincère, et cela en dépit des allusions à l'antiquité païenne, plus discrètes ici au demeurant" (*La poésie religieuse*, p. 145). Bensimon sees Ronsard as rejecting the belief in the resurrection of the body and feels that in the *Hymne* Ronsard does little more than make "un effort de bon écolier pour exposer un point de vue chrétien.... Ce qui devrait nous faire douter de l'authenticité d'une foi chrétienne chez Ronsard" ("Ronsard et la Mort," p. 190). Cohen displays a remarkable insensitivity to the implications of Ronsard's awakening in himself of "la conscience catholique" (*Ronsard*, p. 172) and apparently regards the pagan influence as insurmountable commenting reproachfully, as we have seen (*supra*, n. 10), upon Ronsard's description of Christ's death for us upon the Cross.

> Et chanter son obseque en la façon du Cygne,
> Qui chante son trespas sur les bors Maeandrins.
>   C'est fait j'ay devidé le cours de mes destins,
> J'ay vescu j'ay rendu mon nom assez insigne,
> Ma plume vole au ciel pour estre quelque signe
> Loin des appas mondains qui trompent les plus fins.
>   Heureux qui ne fut onc, plus heureux qui retourne
> En rien comme il estoit, plus heureux qui sejourne
> D'homme fait nouvel ange aupres de Jesuchrist,
>   Laissant pourrir ça bas sa despouille de boüe
> Dont le sort, la fortune, & le destin se joüe,
> Franc des liens du corps pour n'estre qu'un esprit.
>
>   (XVIII, 180-181)

The sonnet moves us by the commingling of both the not quite sorrowful adieu to life and the sick man's appeal for deliverance from fatigue and suffering. The song of the swan is pagan. The life of the senses is evoked. The quest for the 'old' perfection, beauty, and immortality, won through genius and labor, is recalled, and the final disillusionment with the deceptive charm and lure of life itself is clearly stated. Oblivion is preferable to the life of the body. The resolution, however, is expressed through the Christian vision of the duality of man and of his eternal life by the side of the Savior.

The essential role played by the Christian inspiration in much of Ronsard's poetry is evident. It is all the more significant in that it does not occur in isolated, rare passages. The poems in which it is present serve to emphasize the validity of the view of a less rationalistic Ronsard in respect to his vision of man and his destiny. Its aesthetic function and its relationship to Ronsard's poetry in general — from the psychologically taut and complex *Amours* to the calmer philosophical and elegiac musings — still remains to be elucidated adequately. In short, the problem is not to choose between the pagan and the Christian Ronsard; it is, rather, a question of increasing our awareness of the unique, indispensable contribution that the Christian element brings to his poetry.

The Department of Romance Studies Digital Arts and Collaboration Lab at the University of North Carolina at Chapel Hill is proud to support the digitization of the North Carolina Studies in the Romance Languages and Literatures series.

www.ingramcontent.com/pod-product-compliance
Lightning Source LLC
Chambersburg PA
CBHW020422230426
43663CB00007BA/1284